CONTENTS

The Power of the President 4
Naming the Leader 6
Electing the President. 8
Who Can Run? 10
Taking Over 12
Presidential Payment 14
The Oath of Office 16
Commander in Chief 18
Dealing with Other Countries 20
Job Openings 22
The State of the Union 24
Can Presidents Be Punished? 26
A Strong and Balanced Government 28
Glossary 30
For More Information 31
Index 32

WORDS IN THE GLOSSARY APPEAR IN BOLD TYPE THE FIRST TIME THEY ARE USED IN THE TEXT.

THE POWER OF THE PRESIDENT

The president of the United States is sometimes called "the leader of the free world," but how much power does the president really have? The answer is found in the **document** called the U.S. Constitution. Although it was written more than 200 years ago, the Constitution is still used to define the different branches of the U.S. government today.

The Constitution is broken up into pieces called articles, and each article explains part of the government and how the country is supposed to be run. The president's job is explained in Article II.

The president is the head of the executive branch of the U.S. government. Article II established that branch, and it continues to be used today to tell presidents what they can and can't do.

A CLOSER LOOK

ARTICLE NUMBERS IN THE U.S. CONSTITUTION ARE WRITTEN USING ROMAN NUMERALS, SUCH AS ARTICLE II. SMALLER PARTS OF THOSE ARTICLES, CALLED SECTIONS, ARE WRITTEN USING ARABIC NUMERALS, SUCH AS SECTION 2.

THE CONSTITUTION EXPLAINED!
ARTICLE II
BUILDING THE EXECUTIVE BRANCH

BY KATIE KAWA

Gareth Stevens
PUBLISHING

Please visit our website, www.garethstevens.com. For a free color catalog of all our high-quality books, call toll free 1-800-542-2595 or fax 1-877-542-2596.

Library of Congress Cataloging-in-Publication Data

Names: Kawa, Katie, author.
Title: Article II : building the executive branch / Katie Kawa.
Other titles: Article II
Description: New York : Gareth Stevens Publishing, 2021. | Series: The Constitution explained! | Includes index. | Contents: The Power of the President – Naming the Leader – Electing the President – Who Can Run? – Taking Over – Presidential Payment – The Oath of Office – Commander in Chief – Dealing with Other Countries – Job Openings – The State of the Union – Can Presidents Be Punished? – A Strong and Balanced Government
Identifiers: LCCN 2019060195 | ISBN 9781538258569 (library binding) | ISBN 9781538258545 (paperback) | ISBN 9781538258552 (6 Pack)| ISBN 9781538258576 (ebook)
Subjects: LCSH: Presidents–Legal status, laws, etc.–United States–Juvenile literature. | Executive power–United States–Juvenile literature. | United States. Constitution. Article 2–Juvenile literature.
Classification: LCC KF5051 .K39 2020 | DDC 342.73/06–dc23
LC record available at https://lccn.loc.gov/2019060195

First Edition

Published in 2021 by
Gareth Stevens Publishing
111 East 14th Street, Suite 349
New York, NY 10003

Copyright © 2021 Gareth Stevens Publishing

Designer: Sarah Liddell
Editor: Therese Shea

Photo credits: Cover, p. 1 Bloomberg/Contributor/Bloomberg/Getty Images; background texture used throughout Lukasz Szwaj/Shutterstock.com; p. 5 Pgiam/E+/Getty Images; p. 9 PSboom/Shutterstock.com; pp. 11, 15 (top), 27 Chip Somodevilla/Staff/Getty Images News/Getty Images; p. 15 (bottom) SAUL LOEB/Staff/AFP/Getty Images; p. 17 Chicago Tribune/Contributor/Tribune News Service/Getty Images;
p. 19 SABAH ARAR/Staff/AFP/Getty Images; p. 21 HOW HWEE YOUNG/Stringer/AFP/Getty Images; p. 23 Mark Reinstein/Contributor/Corbis News/Getty Images;
p. 25 Xinhua News Agency/Contributor Xinhua News Agency/Getty Images;
p. 29 Mario Tama/Staff/Getty Images News/Getty Images.

All rights reserved. No part of this book may be reproduced in any form without permission in writing from the publisher, except by a reviewer.

Printed in the United States of America

Some of the images in this book illustrate individuals who are models. The depictions do not imply actual situations or events.

CPSIA compliance information: Batch #CS20GS: For further information contact Gareth Stevens, New York, New York at 1-800-542-2595.

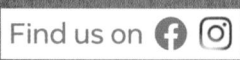

PRESIDENTIAL PRONOUNS

If you look closely at Article II, you'll notice a word is missing: "she." That doesn't mean a woman can't be president! The pronoun "he" was often used instead of "he or she" in writings when the Constitution was written. Women were U.S. citizens back then too—even though they weren't allowed to vote! There are other signs of old styles of writing in the Constitution, such as the practice of capitalizing the first letter of nouns.

SOME PEOPLE, AND EVEN PRESIDENTS, MAY THINK THE U.S. PRESIDENT HAS THE POWER TO DO ANYTHING—BUT ARTICLE II LIMITS THIS POWER!

NAMING THE LEADER

Section 1 of Article II begins by stating, "THE EXECUTIVE POWER SHALL BE VESTED IN A PRESIDENT OF THE UNITED STATES OF AMERICA." This is a formal way of saying that the Constitution gives the president the power that comes with leading the executive branch. Generally, this means that it's the president's job to make sure that the laws are enforced and executed, or carried out.

Before the Constitution, the Articles of Confederation set up the young U.S. government. It created a very weak federal, or national, government, which didn't work well. When the Founding Fathers wrote the Constitution, they knew they had to make the federal government stronger. This included having a leader for the executive branch, whom they called a president.

A CLOSER LOOK

ARTICLE II ALSO TALKS ABOUT THE VICE PRESIDENT, ANOTHER MEMBER OF THE EXECUTIVE BRANCH. OTHER EXECUTIVE BRANCH OFFICIALS INCLUDE THE PRESIDENT'S CABINET—A GROUP OF PEOPLE WHO ADVISE THE PRESIDENT AND LEAD DEPARTMENTS THAT DEAL WITH ISSUES SUCH AS EDUCATION, WAR, AND HOUSING.

TWO TERMS

The Constitution originally stated that a president's term was to last for four years, but there was no limit to how many terms a president could be elected to serve. Nearly all presidents, starting with George Washington, never served for more than two terms. However, Franklin Delano Roosevelt was elected president four times in the 1930s and 1940s! The Twenty-second **Amendment**, passed in 1951, officially stated that a president can only serve two terms in office.

THE FIRST THREE ARTICLES OF THE CONSTITUTION DEFINE THE POWERS OF THE THREE BRANCHES OF THE U.S. GOVERNMENT. THE CONSTITUTION SET UP A SYSTEM OF CHECKS AND BALANCES THAT GIVES EACH BRANCH THE ABILITY TO STOP THE OTHER BRANCHES FROM ABUSING, OR MISUSING, THEIR POWERS.

THE THREE BRANCHES OF U.S. GOVERNMENT

LEGISLATIVE BRANCH
- DEFINED IN ARTICLE I OF THE CONSTITUTION
- MAKES THE LAWS
- INCLUDES MEMBERS OF CONGRESS, WHICH IS MADE UP OF THE SENATE AND HOUSE OF REPRESENTATIVES

EXECUTIVE BRANCH
- DEFINED IN ARTICLE II OF THE CONSTITUTION
- CARRIES OUT AND ENFORCES THE LAWS
- INCLUDES THE PRESIDENT, VICE PRESIDENT, AND OTHER CABINET MEMBERS

JUDICIAL BRANCH
- DEFINED IN ARTICLE III OF THE CONSTITUTION
- INTERPRETS, OR EXPLAINS, THE LAWS
- INCLUDES THE SUPREME COURT AND OTHER FEDERAL COURTS

ELECTING THE PRESIDENT

Article II Section 1 also sets up the process for electing a president. This is known as the Electoral College. U.S. citizens don't vote for the president directly. Instead, they vote for a group of electors. According to Article II, a state's number of electors is **"EQUAL TO THE WHOLE NUMBER OF SENATORS AND REPRESENTATIVES TO WHICH THE STATE MAY BE ENTITLED IN THE CONGRESS."** Then, the electors vote for the president and vice president.

According to Section 1, the person who gets the highest number of votes from the electors is named the president, and the person with the second highest number is the vice president. However, after a tie in the election of 1800, the Twelfth Amendment was passed, stating that electors would cast separate votes for president and vice president.

A CLOSER LOOK

ARTICLE II STATES THAT "CONGRESS MAY DETERMINE THE TIME OF CHUSING [CHOOSING] THE ELECTORS, AND THE DAY ON WHICH THEY SHALL GIVE THEIR VOTES." THEY VOTE IN DECEMBER, AND THEIR **BALLOTS** ARE USUALLY COUNTED ON JANUARY 6.

WHAT THE PEOPLE WANT?

The winner of the electoral vote doesn't always match the winner of the **popular vote**. In the 1800s, Rutherford B. Hayes and Benjamin Harrison won the electoral vote despite losing the popular vote. Then, in 2000, George W. Bush became president because of electoral votes, even though Al Gore won the popular vote. In 2016, Hillary Clinton won the popular vote by more than 2 million votes, but Donald Trump still had enough electoral votes to become president.

THIS ELECTORAL COLLEGE MAP SHOWS THE NUMBER OF ELECTORS IN EACH STATE FOR THE 2020 PRESIDENTIAL ELECTION. ELECTORAL VOTES ARE GIVEN TO THE STATES ACCORDING TO THE RESULTS OF THE U.S. **CENSUS**.

WHO CAN RUN?

Who can run for president? Article II has the answer to that!

Section 1 states, "NO PERSON EXCEPT A NATURAL BORN CITIZEN, OR A CITIZEN OF THE UNITED STATES, AT THE TIME OF THE ADOPTION OF THIS CONSTITUTION, SHALL BE **ELIGIBLE** TO THE OFFICE OF PRESIDENT." This means that a person must have been born a U.S. citizen and can't be an **immigrant** who became a citizen later in life. However, if a person was born somewhere else but became a citizen of the United States by the time the Constitution was adopted in 1788, they could also run for president.

Also according to Section 1, the president must be at least "THE AGE OF THIRTY FIVE YEARS, AND BEEN FOURTEEN YEARS A RESIDENT WITHIN THE UNITED STATES."

BORN IN THE U.S.A.

Barack Obama was elected president in 2008, becoming the first African American to lead the executive branch. However, some people claimed he wasn't a natural-born citizen, which would have made him unable to be president according to Article II. They said he was born in Kenya because that's where his father was from. These claims were untrue; he was born in Hawaii. Many Americans thought Obama was treated in this unfair way because of his race.

ARTICLE II DOESN'T SAY ANYTHING ABOUT WHAT RACE OR GENDER A PERSON MUST BE TO RUN FOR PRESIDENT, WHAT THEIR BACKGROUND SHOULD BE, OR WHAT KIND OF JOB THEY SHOULD HAVE. IN RECENT YEARS, THE PEOPLE RUNNING FOR PRESIDENT REPRESENT A MORE DIVERSE GROUP OF AMERICANS.

A CLOSER LOOK

JOHN F. KENNEDY WAS THE YOUNGEST PERSON TO BE ELECTED PRESIDENT OF THE UNITED STATES. HE WAS 43 YEARS OLD WHEN HE TOOK OFFICE IN 1961.

TAKING OVER

The Founding Fathers planned for many things when they wrote the Constitution. They even had a plan for how to proceed if the president could no longer do the job. Article II explained what to do **"IN CASE OF THE REMOVAL OF THE PRESIDENT FROM OFFICE, OR OF HIS DEATH, RESIGNATION, OR INABILITY TO DISCHARGE [CARRY OUT] THE POWERS AND DUTIES OF THE SAID OFFICE."**

According to the original text of the Constitution, the vice president would take over, but it was unclear if the vice president was supposed to become president or just do the president's job until the next election. The Twenty-fifth Amendment made this clearer. It states that **"THE VICE PRESIDENT SHALL BECOME PRESIDENT"** if the president can't do the job anymore.

FROM VICE PRESIDENT TO PRESIDENT

As of 2020, eight vice presidents have become president because the president died during their time in office. They are John Tyler, Millard Fillmore, Andrew Johnson, Chester Arthur, Theodore Roosevelt, Calvin Coolidge, Harry Truman, and Lyndon B. Johnson. Andrew Johnson, Theodore Roosevelt, and Lyndon B. Johnson took over after the president was assassinated, or killed. Gerald Ford moved from the vice presidency to the presidency because Richard Nixon resigned, or stepped down from his position, in 1974.

PRESIDENTIAL SUCCESSION

- PRESIDENT
- VICE PRESIDENT
- SPEAKER OF THE HOUSE OF REPRESENTATIVES (THE LEADER OF THE HOUSE)
- PRESIDENT PRO TEMPORE OF THE SENATE (OFTEN THE LONGEST SERVING SENATOR FROM THE MAJORITY PARTY WHO'S IN CHARGE OF THE SENATE WHEN THE VICE PRESIDENT ISN'T)
- SECRETARY OF STATE
- SECRETARY OF THE TREASURY
- SECRETARY OF DEFENSE
- ATTORNEY GENERAL
- SECRETARY OF THE INTERIOR
- SECRETARY OF AGRICULTURE
- SECRETARY OF COMMERCE
- SECRETARY OF LABOR
- SECRETARY OF HEALTH AND HUMAN SERVICES
- SECRETARY OF HOUSING AND URBAN DEVELOPMENT
- SECRETARY OF TRANSPORTATION
- SECRETARY OF ENERGY
- SECRETARY OF EDUCATION
- SECRETARY OF VETERANS AFFAIRS
- SECRETARY OF HOMELAND SECURITY

SHOWN HERE IS THE LINE OF PRESIDENTIAL SUCCESSION, OR WHO'S IN LINE TO BECOME PRESIDENT IF THE CURRENT PRESIDENT CAN NO LONGER DO THE JOB. IF ANY OF THESE PEOPLE DON'T MEET THE REQUIREMENTS FOR BEING PRESIDENT, THEY'RE SKIPPED.

A CLOSER LOOK

THE TWENTY-FIFTH AMENDMENT EXPLAINS WHAT TO DO IF THE VICE PRESIDENT CAN NO LONGER DO THE JOB. THE PRESIDENT MUST APPOINT A NEW VICE PRESIDENT, WHO MUST BE APPROVED BY A MAJORITY IN BOTH THE SENATE AND THE HOUSE OF REPRESENTATIVES.

PRESIDENTIAL PAYMENT

Being president is a job, and just like other jobs, people who do it get paid. Article II Section 1 breaks down the president's **"COMPENSATION,"** or payment. It explains that it **"SHALL NEITHER BE ENCREASED [INCREASED] NOR DIMINISHED [LOWERED] DURING THE PERIOD FOR WHICH HE SHALL HAVE BEEN ELECTED."** This means that Congress can't change how much the president is paid during their term.

This section also states that a president can't receive **"ANY OTHER EMOLUMENT FROM THE UNITED STATES, OR ANY OF THEM."** An emolument is a payment, so this means the president can't be paid for anything else or by anyone else outside of the presidential salary. This is a way to make sure states don't unfairly influence presidents by paying them.

GIVING IT AWAY

George Washington didn't want to be paid to be president, but he accepted a salary because it was part of the Constitution. Some other presidents after him chose to give the money they earned to those in need. Herbert Hoover, John F. Kennedy, and Donald Trump gave their salaries to charities. These presidents were very rich men before taking office and didn't need the money, so they chose to help others with it instead.

"NO TITLE OF NOBILITY SHALL BE GRANTED BY THE UNITED STATES: AND NO PERSON HOLDING ANY OFFICE OF PROFIT OR TRUST UNDER THEM, SHALL, **WITHOUT THE CONSENT OF THE CONGRESS,** ACCEPT OF ANY PRESENT, EMOLUMENT, OFFICE, OR TITLE, OF ANY KIND WHATEVER, FROM ANY KING, PRINCE, OR FOREIGN STATE."

CONGRESS DECIDES HOW MUCH TO PAY THE PRESIDENT. AS OF 2020, THE PRESIDENT EARNS $400,000 A YEAR. IN ADDITION, THEY'RE GIVEN $50,000 FOR EXTRA EXPENSES, $19,000 FOR OFFICIAL ENTERTAINMENT COSTS, AND $100,000 FOR TRAVEL.

A CLOSER LOOK

ARTICLE I STATES THAT A PERSON WHO HOLDS A FEDERAL GOVERNMENT OFFICE CAN'T ACCEPT "ANY PRESENT, EMOLUMENT, OFFICE OR TITLE OF ANY KIND WHATEVER FROM ANY KING, PRINCE OR FOREIGN STATE." THIS IS KNOWN AS THE FOREIGN EMOLUMENTS CLAUSE.

THE OATH OF OFFICE

Section 1 of Article II ends with what we now know as the oath of office: "I DO SOLEMNLY SWEAR (OR AFFIRM) THAT I WILL FAITHFULLY EXECUTE THE OFFICE OF PRESIDENT OF THE UNITED STATES, AND WILL TO THE BEST OF MY ABILITY, PRESERVE, PROTECT AND DEFEND THE CONSTITUTION OF THE UNITED STATES."

An oath is a promise, and the oath of office is a promise the president makes on their inauguration day—the day they officially begin their duties as president. They promise to do their best to **uphold** the Constitution and to make sure its laws are guarded and followed.

Every president in U.S. history has taken this oath. Even today, hundreds of years after these words were written, they're still the most important part of a president's inauguration day.

A CLOSER LOOK

MOST PRESIDENTS HAVE ADDED THE PHRASE "SO HELP ME GOD" TO THE END OF THE OATH OF OFFICE. THIS ISN'T IN THE CONSTITUTION. SOME HISTORIANS BELIEVE GEORGE WASHINGTON WAS THE FIRST TO ADD THOSE WORDS, BUT OTHERS BELIEVE IT HAPPENED LATER.

INAUGURATION DAY IN THE CONSTITUTION

Today, the president takes the oath of office in January, but that wasn't always the case. For many years, the presidential inauguration took place in March. However, by the 20th century, many people believed that the time **between Election Day in November and the inauguration of a president in March was too long**. In 1933, the Twentieth Amendment moved the inauguration to January 20. At noon on this day, one presidential term ends, and another begins.

HUNDREDS OF THOUSANDS OF PEOPLE GATHER IN WASHINGTON, DC, TO SEE A NEW PRESIDENT TAKE THE OATH OF OFFICE.

COMMANDER IN CHIEF

Section 2 of Article II outlines the president's duties and powers. It begins with the president's military powers: **"THE PRESIDENT SHALL BE COMMANDER IN CHIEF OF THE ARMY AND NAVY OF THE UNITED STATES."** This means the president is the leader of the U.S. military forces.

Although presidents are the head of the military, they can't declare war on other countries. The Constitution gives that power to Congress. However, the president can ask Congress to declare war for the safety and defense of the country.

In more recent years, the president has used this power over the military to become involved in conflicts around the world. They've sent troops into major conflicts in Korea, Vietnam, Iraq, and Afghanistan, along with smaller conflicts in other countries.

A CLOSER LOOK

CONGRESS HAS OFFICIALLY DECLARED WAR 11 TIMES. THE LAST TIME WAS AGAINST ROMANIA, BULGARIA, AND HUNGARY IN 1942, DURING WORLD WAR II.

THE POWER TO PARDON

Section 2 gives the president the "POWER TO GRANT REPRIEVES AND PARDONS FOR OFFENCES AGAINST THE UNITED STATES." This means they can overturn convictions made in federal or military court. If someone commits a crime and is pardoned, they're no longer guilty under the law. Presidents are also given the power to grant reprieves. A reprieve is a delay in a sentence, often to give someone time to prove their innocence. These powers are a check on the judicial branch.

ALTHOUGH WE OFTEN CALL RECENT MILITARY CONFLICTS "WARS," SUCH AS THE VIETNAM WAR, GULF WAR, AND IRAQ WAR, THESE WEREN'T ACTUAL WARS DECLARED BY CONGRESS. INSTEAD, THESE WERE MILITARY ENGAGEMENTS LED BY THE EXECUTIVE BRANCH.

DEALING WITH OTHER COUNTRIES

The president doesn't only deal with foreign countries in times of conflict. Presidents also work with other countries to make peace and to work toward common goals. According to Article II, the president has the **"POWER, BY AND WITH THE ADVICE AND CONSENT OF THE SENATE, TO MAKE TREATIES, PROVIDED TWO THIRDS OF THE SENATORS PRESENT CONCUR [AGREE]."** Treaties are formal agreements with other countries, and they're so important that the president alone can't make them. The president must be advised by the Senate, and the Senate must approve the treaty.

In some cases, the president can make "executive agreements" with other countries without the Senate's approval or advice. However, they're generally about issues less important than the treaties involving issues such as war and peace, which require the Senate's approval.

A CLOSER LOOK

SOMETIMES THE SENATE REJECTS A TREATY. FOR EXAMPLE, THE SENATE REJECTED THE 1919 TREATY OF VERSAILLES THAT ENDED WORLD WAR I BECAUSE PRESIDENT WOODROW WILSON DIDN'T INCLUDE SENATORS WHEN MAKING THE TREATY.

THE FACE OF THE NATION

The president often represents the United States when dealing with other countries. Article II states that the president "SHALL RECEIVE AMBASSADORS," or people who represent other countries. The president also meets with world leaders at the White House and travels to other countries to make executive agreements and to strengthen relationships. Diplomacy—working with other countries—is an important part of the president's job, even though it's not mentioned much in the Constitution.

Sometimes it's not clear if an agreement with another country should be seen as an executive agreement or a treaty. For example, when Barack Obama brought the United States into the Paris agreement to fight climate change, some senators believed he should have sought their approval.

JOB OPENINGS

It's the president's job to fill many positions in the U.S. government, including members of the cabinet and ambassadors. When the president names someone for one of these jobs, it's called an appointment. However, these appointments, like treaties, can only be made with **"THE ADVICE AND CONSENT OF THE SENATE."**

Article II also gives the president the power to nominate **"JUDGES OF THE SUPREME COURT."** When there's an opening on the U.S. Supreme Court, the president must nominate a judge to fill it, but the Senate must approve the person.

Article II doesn't say anything about removing people from appointed positions. Different presidents have had different methods for dealing with this issue. For example, some have asked advisers and cabinet members to resign rather than firing them.

A CLOSER LOOK

SUPREME COURT JUSTICES SERVE FOR LIFE AFTER THEY'RE APPOINTED. A SEAT ON THE BENCH ONLY OPENS FOR A NEW NOMINEE AFTER A JUSTICE DIES, STEPS DOWN, OR IS REMOVED FROM OFFICE.

DEEP DIVISIONS

American politics today reflects a deep divide between members of the Republican Party and members of the Democratic Party. This division reveals itself when the Senate needs to approve a president's nominee for the Supreme Court. For example, in 2016, Barack Obama, a Democrat, nominated Merrick Garland to the Supreme Court. However, Republicans in the Senate wouldn't approve any nominee until after the 2016 presidential election. After Republican Donald Trump was elected, the Senate approved his nominee, Neil Gorsuch.

SUPREME COURT NOMINEES ATTEND HEARINGS IN THE SENATE WHERE THEY'RE ASKED MANY QUESTIONS ABOUT THEIR LIFE AND WORK. JUSTICE RUTH BADER GINSBURG WAS APPOINTED TO THE SUPREME COURT DURING BILL CLINTON'S PRESIDENCY.

THE STATE OF THE UNION

One of the most important speeches the president gives each year is called the State of the Union Address. This speech is actually a constitutional requirement for presidents. Article II Section 3 begins by stating, **"[THE PRESIDENT] SHALL FROM TIME TO TIME GIVE TO THE CONGRESS INFORMATION OF THE STATE OF THE UNION, AND RECOMMEND TO THEIR CONSIDERATION SUCH MEASURES AS HE SHALL JUDGE NECESSARY AND EXPEDIENT."** During this speech, which now is shown on television for all to watch, the president addresses Congress to report what has been achieved and to gather support for important issues.

Section 3 also states that the president can call for special sessions of Congress outside their normal meeting time. It ends by stating that the president must **"TAKE CARE THAT THE LAWS BE FAITHFULLY EXECUTED."**

A CLOSER LOOK

AT TIMES IN U.S. HISTORY, THE STATE OF THE UNION ADDRESS WAS DELIVERED IN WRITING AND NOT IN PERSON. HOWEVER, IT'S BEEN DELIVERED IN PERSON SINCE THE 1980s. BILL CLINTON HOLDS THE RECORD FOR THE LONGEST STATE OF THE UNION ADDRESS DELIVERED IN PERSON.

EXECUTIVE ORDERS

Presidents have claimed that Article II allows them to issue executive orders. These orders are like federal laws. Presidents have stated that these orders help them **"TAKE CARE THAT THE LAWS BE FAITHFULLY EXECUTED."** One of the most famous is the Emancipation Proclamation, which Abraham Lincoln issued in 1863 to free the slaves in the **Confederacy** during the American Civil War. Today, presidents may issue hundreds of executive orders during their time in office.

THE STATE OF THE UNION ADDRESS ALLOWS PRESIDENTS TO TELL CONGRESS AND THE AMERICAN PEOPLE HOW THEY FEEL ABOUT THE DIRECTION THE COUNTRY IS HEADING IN AND WHAT THEY HOPE TO ACCOMPLISH DURING THE NEXT YEAR.

CAN PRESIDENTS BE PUNISHED?

Presidents are powerful people. If they misuse their power, Section 4 of Article II gives Congress the power to impeach them, which means charge them with misconduct. It states, **"THE PRESIDENT, VICE PRESIDENT AND ALL CIVIL OFFICERS OF THE UNITED STATES, SHALL BE REMOVED FROM OFFICE ON IMPEACHMENT FOR, AND CONVICTION OF, TREASON, BRIBERY, OR OTHER HIGH CRIMES AND MISDEMEANORS."**

Treason is the act of betraying your country, and bribery involves offering money to influence someone's actions. Other abuses of power and crimes can also lead to impeachment.

The House of Representatives votes on impeachment. If they impeach the president, a Senate trial is held to decide if the president should be removed from office. Even though there's a trial, impeachment is a political process rather than a legal one.

A CLOSER LOOK

CONGRESS HAS THE POWER TO IMPEACH MEMBERS OF THE OTHER BRANCHES OF THE U.S. GOVERNMENT. THE MAJORITY OF OFFICIALS WHO'VE BEEN IMPEACHED HAVE BEEN JUDGES.

WHO'S BEEN IMPEACHED?

No president has been removed from office by the impeachment process yet. The House of Representatives has impeached three U.S. presidents so far—Andrew Johnson, Bill Clinton, and Donald Trump. The Senate didn't vote to remove them from office, though. President Richard Nixon resigned in 1974 before he could be impeached. Also, Article II Section 2 states that presidents aren't allowed to pardon themselves "IN CASES OF IMPEACHMENT."

IMPEACHMENT IS ANOTHER EXAMPLE OF THE CHECKS AND BALANCES BETWEEN THE BRANCHES OF THE U.S. GOVERNMENT. THE LEGISLATIVE BRANCH, CONGRESS, CAN "CHECK" THE ABUSE OF POWER BY THE EXECUTIVE BRANCH.

A STRONG AND BALANCED GOVERNMENT

The U.S. Constitution is the oldest written national constitution still in use. More than 200 years ago, the Founding Fathers created a document that was clear enough to build a lasting government but also open enough to different interpretations that it could still apply to a changing world.

For example, parts of Article II outline clear powers of the presidency, such as appointing Supreme Court justices, but other parts aren't as clear. This can lead to questions about how much power the president really has.

These questions are often answered by the Supreme Court, and Congress can also put a check on presidential power. Article II has worked with the other parts of the Constitution to keep the U.S. government strong and balanced hundreds of years after the nation was founded.

A CLOSER LOOK

MORE THAN HALF OF ALL PRESIDENTS HAVE BEEN LAWYERS, SO THEY'VE HAD A GOOD UNDERSTANDING OF THE CONSTITUTION. BARACK OBAMA TAUGHT STUDENTS ABOUT CONSTITUTIONAL LAW AT THE UNIVERSITY OF CHICAGO LAW SCHOOL BEFORE HE BECAME PRESIDENT.

VETO POWER

One of the most important powers the president has isn't stated in Article II: Presidents have the power to veto bills passed by Congress, which means they don't sign the bill into law. This power is granted in Article I Section 7. This section states that any bill "SHALL BE APPROVED BY [THE PRESIDENT], OR BEING DISAPPROVED BY HIM, SHALL BE REPASSED BY [A VOTE OF] TWO THIRDS OF THE SENATE AND HOUSE OF REPRESENTATIVES."

UNDERSTANDING THE CONSTITUTION, ESPECIALLY ARTICLE II, IS AN IMPORTANT PART OF BEING AN INFORMED CITIZEN AND VOTER. WHEN A CITIZEN VOTES FOR THE PRESIDENT OF THE UNITED STATES, THEY SHOULD THINK ABOUT THE PERSON WHO COULD BEST HANDLE THE DUTIES AND POWERS DESCRIBED IN THIS DOCUMENT.

GLOSSARY

amendment: a change or addition to a constitution

ballot: a sheet of paper listing candidates' names and used for voting

census: the official process of counting the number of people and collecting information about them in a town, city, or country

clause: a separate part of a legal document

Confederacy: the group of Southern states that broke away from the Union during the American Civil War to form the Confederate States of America

diverse: differing from each other

document: a formal piece of writing

eligible: qualified to do something

expedient: easy and quick

immigrant: one who comes to a country to settle there

misdemeanor: a lesser crime

popular vote: the choice expressed through the votes cast by eligible voters as opposed to the Electoral College

uphold: to strengthen something or keep it going

FOR MORE INFORMATION

BOOKS

Kellaher, Karen. *The Presidency: Why It Matters to You.* New York, NY: Children's Press, 2020.

Miller, Derek. *Executive Orders.* New York, NY: Cavendish Square Publishing, 2019.

Nelson, Kristen Rajczak. *U.S. Constitution.* New York, NY: PowerKids Press, 2017.

WEBSITES

Branches of the U.S. Government
www.usa.gov/branches-of-government
This website explains the three branches of the U.S. government and their powers.

The Constitution of the United States
www.archives.gov/founding-docs/constitution
The National Archives website features the full text of the document.

Presidents
www.whitehouse.gov/about-the-white-house/presidents/
This official White House website has facts about each U.S. president.

Publisher's note to educators and parents: Our editors have carefully reviewed these websites to ensure that they are suitable for students. Many websites change frequently, however, and we cannot guarantee that a site's future contents will continue to meet our high standards of quality and educational value. Be advised that students should be closely supervised whenever they access the internet.

INDEX

ambassadors 21, 22
appointments 13, 22, 23, 28
Articles of Confederation 6
cabinet 6, 22
checks and balances 7, 27
Congress 8, 14, 15, 18, 19, 24, 25, 26, 27, 28, 29
crime 19, 26
Democratic Party 23
election 8, 9, 12, 23
Electoral College 8, 9
Emancipation Proclamation 25
executive order 25
Founding Fathers 6, 12, 28
House of Representatives 13, 26, 27, 29
impeachment 26, 27
inauguration 16, 17
judicial branch 19
justices 22, 28
legislative branch 27
military 18, 19

Nixon, Richard 12, 27
oath of office 16, 17
Obama, Barack 10, 21, 23, 28
pardons 19, 27
Paris Agreement 21
payment 14
Republican Party 23
Roosevelt, Franklin Delano 7
Senate 13, 20, 22, 23, 26, 27, 29
State of the Union 24, 25
succession 13
terms 7, 14, 17
treaties 20, 22
Trump, Donald 9, 14, 23, 27
veto 29
vice president 6, 8, 12, 13
war 6, 18, 19, 20
Washington, George 7, 14, 16

32